African-American
Soldiers

Vietnam War Soldiers

Neil Super

Twenty-First Century Books

A Division of Henry Holt and Company New York

PHOTO CREDITS

cover: flag by Fred J. Eckert/FPG International; photo courtesy of UPI/Bettmann. **3,4:** National Archives. **9:** UPI/Bettmann. **14:** AP/Wide World Photos. **16, 20, 22, 23:** UPI/Bettmann. **25:** Bettmann. **27:** National Archives. **31:** UPI/Bettmann. **33:** AP/Wide World Photos. **34, 38, 39:** UPI/Bettmann. **44:** AP/Wide World Photos. **50, 53, 58, 66:** UPI/Bettmann. **71:** AP/Wide World Photos. **75:** UPI/Bettmann.

Twenty-First Century Books
A Division of Henry Holt and Company, Inc.
115 West 18th Street
New York, NY 10011

Henry Holt® and colophon are registered trademarks of Henry Holt and Company, Inc.
Publishers since 1866

Text Copyright © 1993 by Neil Super
All rights reserved.
Published in Canada by Fitzhenry & Whiteside Ltd.,
195 Allstate Parkway, Markham, Ontario L3R 4T8

Library of Congress Cataloging-in-Publication Data

Super, Neil.
Vietnam War soldiers / Neil Super.
p.   cm. — (African-American soldiers)
Includes bibliographical references and index.
Summary: Focuses on the experiences of African-American soldiers in the Vietnam War, experiences that reflected and amplified the struggle for civil rights in America during this same time period.
1. Vietnamese Conflict, 1961-1975—Afro-Americans—Juvenile literature.
2. Afro-Americans—Civil rights—Juvenile literature. 3. United States—Race relations—Juvenile literature. [1. Afro-American soldiers.
2. Vietnamese Conflict, 1961-1975—Afro-Americans.
3. Afro-Americans—Civil rights. 4. Race relations.]
I. Title. II. Series.
DS559.8.B55B37   1993
959.704'31—dc20 93-10626   CIP AC

ISBN 0-8050-2307-0
First Edition—1993

Printed in the United States of America
All first editions are printed on acid-free paper ∞.

10 9 8 7 6 5 4 3 2 1

Contents

Chapter 1

Black or White, I Would Have Done the Same

The wounded man cried, "Mother." He was lying in a field in a country ten thousand miles from home. Enemy soldiers fired feverishly from their concealed positions behind nearby trees, trying to finish the man off. His fellow marines, pinned down by the furious assault, could do nothing to help him.

"Mother," the marine cried again. Fifty yards away, crouching beside his commanding officer, Sergeant Major Edgar A. Huff heard the man's cries and stood to go to him. "No, no," the colonel said as bullets flew all around them. "Just wait."

"Sorry, Colonel," Huff replied over his shoulder. The six-foot-six, forty-eight-year-old African-American soldier had already taken off through the open field, toward the stricken marine.

By the time Sergeant Major Huff reached the

A soldier on a search-and-destroy mission

wounded man, he'd been knocked down twice by bullets that hit his helmet. He threw his body over the fallen marine just as a grenade exploded, ripping into the protective "flak" jacket Huff wore and embedding metal fragments into his shoulder and arm.

Nearby marines rallied with a furious burst of return fire, enough to subdue the enemy while the colonel himself brought a stretcher out. He and Huff carried the wounded man—who was white—to safety. Despite his own wounds, Huff refused to go to the hospital. His men needed him.

"I knew I might get killed saving a white boy," Huff later said. "But he was my man. That's what mattered. Black or white, I would have done the same even if I got shot to hell in the process."

Ed Huff had known pain in his lifetime. He'd grown up poor in the Deep South, in Alabama, where African Americans could expect little in the way of equal opportunity or justice. His father passed away when Huff was six. After that, Huff's mother supported them by working for white families for three dollars a week. Huff dropped out of school at fifteen, when his mother got sick, and went to work for a steel company. Each day he walked four miles to work.

One night when he was about ten years old

Ed Huff heard car horns blowing outside. "The Ku Klux is comin'," his grandfather said. The Ku Klux Klan was a secret society of racist whites that terrorized African Americans with violence and threats while wearing robes and hoods to conceal their identities. That night, as the terrified boy hid under a bed, the Klan took away an African-American neighbor, tied the man to a tree, and whipped him.

In 1942, when Ed Huff signed up, he was one of the first fifty African Americans accepted by the all-white Marine Corps. At this time the armed forces were still segregated—whites and blacks were kept separate from one another. "We had our own barracks, our own infantry, our own tanks, our own guns," Huff recalled. "It couldn't have been more segregated. Of course, the officers was white."

When Huff reported to training camp, it was the first time he had ever left Alabama. He spent his first Christmas as a marine in jail. White military policemen (MPs) had arrested him for impersonating a marine as he made his way home on leave. "What you doin' with that uniform on?" the skeptical MPs had demanded.

With World War II raging, Ed Huff and his fellow marines were eager to join the fight. One night a white general who had fought in the Pacific came to Huff's all-black camp to speak. The men were excited—they'd never seen a general up close, and they wanted to hear about the war from someone who had been there. "I've been fighting through the jungles," the general said. "But I didn't realize there was a war going on until I came back to the United States. When I come back . . . and when I see *you people* wearing *our* uniforms, then I know there's a war going on."

Ed Huff vividly remembered the general's speech and the effect it had on the men. "You never saw so many Coke bottles fly," he said. "Knocked him down. And there was a riot that night. The first black riot in Marine Corps history."

Huff rose through the ranks quickly. Less than two years after his enlistment, he was the sergeant in charge of training all the African-American marines for combat. When they were finally shipped out to the Pacific, however, the men learned that their only duty would be providing supplies for all-white combat units.

By the 1950s the armed forces were integrated. Black and white soldiers fought side by side. Ed Huff saw combat in the Korean War. He was eventually promoted to sergeant major, the highest of the enlisted ranks. Even then, however, he continued to encounter racism. Each incident hurt Huff deeply. "If there's ever a man should be prejudiced as far as the white man is concerned," he once said, "I should be. 'Cause some of these officers kicked me every which way but loose.

"But I never let any of these things make me prejudiced right back," he continued. "Especially in combat. Especially in Vietnam. I am the sergeant major. I take care of all of my men, black and white."

A wounded soldier is rescued while under heavy shelling

This book tells the story of African-American soldiers in Vietnam. It tells about people like Sergeant Major Edgar A. Huff, whose willingness to risk his life for another earned him a medal for gallantry. Twenty African Americans won the Medal of Honor, America's highest award for bravery in battle, for their extraordinary feats in Vietnam. Tens of thousands of others, however, performed daily acts of courage and self-sacrifice that went unrewarded—except for the gratitude of their fellow soldiers.

This book is also a story about opportunity and achievement. Finally allowed to work and compete with whites on an equal basis, African Americans served their country in an unprecedented variety of roles in Vietnam. While their achievements in that bitterly divisive war have too often been overlooked, the fact is that in Vietnam, African Americans proved once again that whatever the crisis, they could be called upon to serve America well.

Sadly, this book also tells about bigotry and injustice. The war, fought at a time of historic change and upheaval in American society, diverted America's attention from sorely needed social programs and improvements in race relations. In Vietnam, African Americans faced not only a foreign enemy but the additional enemy of racism as well.

Deeply ingrained in American society since the days of slavery, racist attitudes followed African Americans to Vietnam. Racism greeted them when they came home, too, embittering many who knew they deserved better. Significantly, the war marked the first time in the nation's history that a large number of African-American leaders urged their people not to go to war for America.

Hundreds of thousands of African Americans did go to Vietnam, for a variety of reasons. This is their story.

Chapter 2

To Prevent Further Aggression

Vietnam is an S-shaped country that sits on the eastern edge of the peninsula known as Indochina. With more than twelve hundred miles of coastline along the South China Sea forming its eastern boundary, Vietnam is just slightly smaller than California. To its north lies massive China. To the west, across the Annamite Mountain Range, are two other Indo-Chinese nations—Laos and Cambodia.

Vietnam's geography is dominated by dense tropical jungles and fertile river valleys. In the northern part of the country are the Red River Delta and the capital city of Hanoi. The ancient capital of long-gone emperors, Hue (pronounced "whay"), is located in the central region. The southern part of the big S that is Vietnam is sometimes referred to as the Mekong Delta area, for it is there that the Mekong River splits into several smaller streams that provide water to one of the finest agricultural treasures in Asia.

By the time the United States became involved in the Vietnam conflict, that country had already endured centuries of intervention by other peoples, including the Chinese and the French. Often outnumbered, the fierce Vietnamese learned early in their history to avoid large battles where they could be wiped out by superior enemy forces. Instead, the Vietnamese relied on surprise attacks and rapid movements that tended to wear larger armies down, weakening their defenses. This style of fighting is known as "guerrilla warfare."

During the 1950s, certain Vietnamese called "nationalists" had driven the French from the northern part of Vietnam. The most famous nationalist leader was a man called Ho Chi Minh. Ho Chi Minh believed strongly in the communist system of government and committed himself to teaching his countrymen about communism. Over the years he gained many supporters among the Vietnamese.

When the French were driven from the north, the world's most powerful nations decided that Vietnam should be temporarily divided in the middle. The communists would control the northern half and an independent state, called the Republic

Ngo Dinh Diem

of South Vietnam, was established in the south, under the leadership of Ngo Dinh Diem (pronounced "No Din Yem").

The United States did not like the fact that the North Vietnamese were communists. U.S. leaders feared the spread of communism around the world, believing that it was a threat to democracy and a direct challenge to America's position as a major world power. For that reason, the United States refused to recognize the government of North Vietnam.

Under the agreement known as the Geneva Accords, elections were to be held in 1956 to reunite Vietnam under a single government. Afraid that the popular Ho Chi Minh would win, and all of Vietnam would be under communist rule, the United States did not join in this part of the Geneva Accords. Diem, also fearful of Ho Chi Minh's popularity, saw to it that the elections were never held.

Because Diem was strongly anticommunist, the United States supported him despite his reputation as a harsh, oppressive leader. His policies angered Ho Chi Minh's supporters in South Vietnam, known as the "Vietcong," which means "communist Vietnamese." The Vietcong supported Ho Chi Minh's efforts to unify the country, and fought the Diem government using the same guerrilla warfare techniques that had driven the French from northern Vietnam.

As the Vietcong grew bolder and Diem's popularity faded, United States president John F. Kennedy made it known that American support of South Vietnam depended on Diem's ability to gain the trust and support of his people. This was not to be. In 1963 Diem was removed from power in a rebellion called a "coup" (pronounced "koo"). The Vietcong and the North Vietnamese used the confusion caused by the coup to attack South Vietnam across the border.

Just weeks after Diem was ousted from power, President Kennedy was assassinated in the United States. As Vice President Lyndon B. Johnson took office as the new president, he realized that the government in South Vietnam was facing an increasing threat from the north. Determined to stop the communists, Johnson ordered supplies and U.S. military advisers sent to Vietnam. He also sent warships to patrol the Vietnamese coastline.

On August 2, 1964, a U.S. ship was attacked off the coast of North Vietnam. President Johnson used this incident to persuade Congress to give him the authority to respond to "any armed attack against the armed forces of the United States and to prevent further aggression." Johnson ordered even more advisers and supplies sent to Vietnam.

By the end of 1964, there were 23,500 U.S. military personnel in Vietnam. Most served as advisers to the Army of the Republic of South Vietnam, known to the Americans as ARVN (pronounced "Arvun"). As fighting between the ARVN and the Vietcong increased, American troops took a more active role.

In March 1965, in response to the deaths of

U.S. Marines instruct ARVN soldiers at a firing range

American servicemen at the hands of the Vietcong, President Johnson ordered the Air Force to begin bombing targets in North Vietnam. Within a week, the first American combat troops, U.S. Marines, arrived in South Vietnam. By that summer they were conducting their own military operations against the Vietcong. America's war in Vietnam had begun.

Chapter 3

Proud to Be Part of It

The armed forces of the 1960s were one of the few integrated institutions in American society. As a result, when the United States first intervened in Vietnam its military ranks included a large number of African Americans, most of whom had joined to take advantage of opportunities not available in the civilian world. For them, the chance for equal opportunity was well worth the risk of being in combat.

Like their white counterparts, the African Americans who served in Vietnam came from all walks of life and were there for a variety of reasons. Career soldiers like Ed Huff and Army medic Lawrence Joel had made the military their profession. Joel, from North Carolina, was thirty-eight years old when he reported for duty in Vietnam. The father of two was a twenty-year Army veteran. He had joined the Army, he recalled, because "as a Negro, you couldn't make it really big in the world."

Charles Rogers, the son of a West Virginia coal miner, had served fifteen years in the Army when he arrived in Vietnam. The ambitious officer volunteered for duty in Vietnam. "I wanted the combat experience and I felt it was imperative to my career to get a combat command," he later recalled.

The average age of a combat soldier in Vietnam was nineteen. Seventeen-year-old Reginald Edwards from Louisiana, the first in his family to graduate from high school, couldn't afford college. His slight build hurt Edwards's chances of finding work in the fields around his hometown. "I only weighed 117 pounds," he recalled, "and nobody's gonna hire me to work for them. So the only thing left to do was go into the service." Edwards joined the Marine Corps in 1963. His mother had to sign his enlistment papers since he wasn't yet eighteen. He arrived in Vietnam in 1965.

Milton Lee Olive enlisted in the Army in 1964, before his senior year of high school. His father wanted Olive to finish school but agreed to let him enlist when he saw how much the young man wanted to join. Seeking adventure beyond his Chicago neighborhood, Olive also arrived in Vietnam in 1965. He quickly became a combat veteran.

Robert Mountain, who volunteered for the Army shortly after beginning college, never

Milton Lee Olive, III

expected to end up in Vietnam. He was a trombone player and wanted nothing more than to play in the Army band. A few days at boot camp convinced Mountain that the Army was not for him. "I called my mother," he remembered, "and I said, 'Mama, I don't think I want to be in the Army. I want to go back to school.'" Mountain auditioned for the Army band but was not accepted. In June 1968, he was sent to Vietnam as a combat soldier.

Patriotism, adventure and the opportunity for success in the military were not the only reasons large numbers of African Americans served in Vietnam. As it had in past wars, the U.S. government required young men to serve in the military through a process known as the "draft." All men of a certain age who were not enrolled in college were eligible to be drafted. During the Vietnam War over twenty-six million men were of draft age. But many never served because they received a college deferment. As a result, many of the over two million men who were drafted were those who could not afford college.

Charles Cato, an African American from New York, was working as a jeweler's apprentice when he learned he'd been drafted in 1965. Entering the military meant giving up his trade—and his freedom—and Cato was not pleased. "I guess I just had to go though," he said later, "and so I went."

In 1965, Harold Bryant's family was unable to afford his college expenses, and so the twenty-year-old African American had dropped out and gotten a job. "About eight months later," he recalled, "two guys I went to high school with got drafted by the Marines." Bryant figured his turn was coming. "So I joined the Army," he continued, "so I could get a choice."

While most draftees accepted their orders, particularly in the early years of the war, there were some who did not. For those who were not deferred or disqualified, the choices were to seek an exemption, usually based on religious reasons, or risk prison for evading the draft. During the war, over fifteen million men were either deferred, disqualified, or exempted. Over half a million others became "draft dodgers," some fleeing to Canada to escape the consequences of draft evasion.

Muhammad Ali, the heavyweight boxing champion, was perhaps the most famous African American to seek exemption as a "conscientious objector" due to his Muslim beliefs. Ali was convicted of draft evasion in 1967 and stripped of his boxing title after refusing to go to Vietnam. In 1971, the Supreme Court overturned the conviction, and Ali eventually made a successful return to boxing.

Muhammad Ali speaking at a Black Muslim meeting after refusing induction into the Army

Army private Winstel R. Belton's situation was a bit different. Belton had been drafted in 1964 and was serving in the Army when his unit was ordered to Vietnam in 1965. Belton, a former civil rights worker, had grave doubts about whether African Americans should serve in Vietnam. He refused to accept his orders. The graduate of Arizona State University and former football player staged a hunger strike to protest the war. The Army jailed him and scheduled a military trial, called a court-martial.

Winstel R. Belton

Regardless of how they felt when the war was over, most soldiers in the early years simply accepted the fact that America had sent them to do a job. "When I came to Vietnam," remembered Harold Bryant, "I thought we were helping another country to develop a nation." Some, like African-American pilot Norman McDaniel, were glad to be there. "When I heard that we were going to Thailand for combat missions against North Vietnam," said McDaniel, a captain in the Air Force, "I felt good, really proud to be part of it." Others weren't so enthusiastic. "I really didn't have an opinion of the war at first," remembered Charles Strong, who was drafted and served in the Army. "I was praying that the war would bypass me."

African Americans have fought in every U.S. war since the American Revolution. At first denied the opportunity to serve, African Americans eventually made up about 10 percent of the Union Army in the Civil War, in which approximately thirty-eight thousand black soldiers died and between sixteen and twenty-three won the Medal of Honor. (Sources vary.) All-black units so distinguished themselves in battle that even bigoted white soldiers paid them grudging respect. Between the end of the Civil War and World War I, the Buffalo Soldiers of the 9th and 10th Cavalry fought desperate battles in the American West against fierce Indian tribes such as the Apache.

The armed forces of the World War I era were not much different from American society at that time. "Jim Crow" laws, rules that promoted racial segregation, had long prevented African Americans from enjoying the benefits of American citizenship. This was especially true in the South, where everything from jails, to movie theaters, park benches, and water fountains was kept separate for blacks and whites. The Navy's version of Jim Crow meant that most African-American sailors worked as cooks and dishwashers. The Army assigned most of its African Americans to perform manual labor, while the Marine Corps simply refused to accept them at all.

During World War I more than 367,000 African Americans loyally served their country, despite the fact that they were treated as second-class citizens. When World War II broke out in 1939, there were about 4,000 African Americans on active duty in the entire armed forces. African Americans once more rushed to defend their country, as 2.5 million volunteered for service. Again, however, discrimination limited the contributions of most African Americans largely to manual labor or kitchen duties.

During World War II, some segregated units of African Americans were given a chance to fight. The famous "Tuskegee Airmen" disproved the Army's claim that blacks could not fly in combat as well as white pilots, as they won a major victory over enemy fliers in Europe. A unit of black military truck drivers nicknamed the "Redball Express" won fame for keeping combat soldiers at the battlefront supplied with ammunition, rations, and other essentials in spite of difficult wartime conditions.

Black troops ate in segregated mess halls during World War II

Even before the start of World War II, African Americans had protested against the segregation of the armed forces. Having fought for their country, they were no longer willing to accept second class status. Influential leaders, both black and white, pressured the government to end segregation and give African Americans equal opportunities in the armed forces. While many military leaders resisted the idea, others realized that Jim Crow weakened America's overall military strength. As a result, in 1948 President Harry S Truman ordered the military to integrate.

By 1950, the recently formed Air Force had taken major steps toward integration. The Army, however, lagged behind. While African-American pilots such as Benjamin O. Davis, Jr., and Daniel "Chappie" James, Jr., were finally allowed to serve on an equal basis with whites during the Korean War, many black infantrymen faced continuing segregation and inequality. As the Korean War continued, however, the Army saw how much equal treatment improved the performance and morale of black soldiers. By 1954, equal treatment of African Americans was official Army policy.

Coming home from Korea, African-American veterans found that despite the changes in the armed forces, little had changed in America. They were still denied equal education, employment,

Daniel "Chappie" James, Jr.

housing, and even the right to vote. Thousands remained in the armed forces for the equal opportunity they found there. Many of these men and women, professional soldiers, were in the ranks when the United States made its fateful decision to intervene in Vietnam.

As the Vietnam War began, America's black warriors dutifully answered their country's call to serve, as they had throughout U.S. history. Once again, they hoped that their loyal and willing service to America would earn them the benefits of equal rights and respect back home. Newly won civil rights and the complete integration of the military seemed to promise a better life in America after the war. While some in the African-American community were troubled by America's involvement in Vietnam, many others were optimistic about the future.

First, however, there was a war to be fought. In Vietnam, African Americans would both distinguish themselves and pay a heavy price.

Chapter 4

An Inspiration to All

By the end of December 1965, there were over 184,000 U.S. troops in Vietnam, 21,519 of whom were African Americans. The United States was taking over the war from the ARVN. Already 1,363 Americans had lost their lives. Another 7,645 had been wounded. Of the dead, 237 were black soldiers. These numbers would increase dramatically as the months passed.

Despite having more and better weapons and supplies than the enemy, for U.S. troops the ground war quickly grew frustrating. The U.S. commander in Vietnam, General William C. Westmoreland, had devised a "search-and-destroy" strategy with the goal of killing as many enemy soldiers as possible. The idea was to rid an area of Vietcong and then provide the local people with food, medicine, and protection. In this way, the Americans hoped to win the trust and loyalty of the people and decrease the communists' influence.

"You can kill ten of my men for one I kill of yours," Ho Chi Minh had once warned the French, "but even at those odds, you will lose and I will win." Ho Chi Minh's army consisted of millions of soldiers—both Vietcong guerrillas and regular North Vietnamese soldiers, called NVA, who flooded into South Vietnam. "We would fight for a hill all day," remembered Harold Bryant, "spend two days or two nights there, and then abandon the hill. Then maybe two, three months later, we would have to come back and retake the same piece of territory."

The war had no front line. The enemy could be anywhere at any time. Because of this, American troops found themselves scattered throughout the country, often moving rapidly from place to place by helicopter. In the early stages of the war, most of the fighting between U.S. troops and the Vietcong occurred in the central highlands of South Vietnam. Here, the thick jungles and lack of roads presented formidable obstacles to U.S. troops on search-and-destroy missions. The jungle was ideally suited for guerrilla warfare—the enemy's hit-and-run fighting style.

Further complicating the fight against the Vietcong was the difficulty American troops had in identifying them. Unlike the NVA, the Vietcong wore no uniforms, dressing instead in the traditional black pajama-like clothing that all peasants wore. By day, the Vietcong blended in with the rest of the citizens of South Vietnam—working in the fields and using the villages as places to store weapons and to hide from the Americans. At night, the Vietcong went out to fight. "Any Vietnamese out at night was the enemy," recalled Reginald Edwards.

American troops also fought the Vietcong farther south, in the Mekong Delta near Saigon, and patrolled the dense jungles and hills of the border

A soldier on patrol along the Mekong Delta

area between South and North Vietnam. This area was known as the "Demilitarized Zone," or "DMZ," because there was supposed to be no fighting there. It was here that U.S. troops were more likely to encounter not Vietcong but the better-trained and better-equipped NVA soldiers.

Whether career soldiers, patriotic volunteers, or draftees, the majority of the African-American fighting men in Vietnam found themselves in the thick of the ground war, with Army or Marine combat units. Charles Cato served as a rifleman in the infantry, the ground units known among soldiers as "grunts." He was a "tunnel rat," a soldier whose small size and agility enabled him to crawl through the underground tunnels the enemy built, searching for Vietcong. "I didn't mind," he said of this risky duty. "I liked the job. I found it exciting."

African Americans served in all aspects of the ground campaign. David Tuck, from Cleveland, was a radio operator in the central highlands of Vietnam. Dwight Johnson, a former altar boy and Explorer scout from Detroit's worst ghetto, was a tank driver. Harold Bryant, nicknamed "Lightbulb" as he grew up because he was always full of ideas, was a combat engineer who specialized in disarming mines and booby traps.

The chance to prove themselves, as well as

U.S. Marines in the jungle just south of the Demilitarized Zone

32

the promise of higher pay, led African Americans like Milton Olive to join elite combat units such as the Army's 173rd Airborne Brigade. These paratroopers, called "Sky Soldiers," would parachute into enemy territory and fight fierce battles, often outnumbered. The Sky Soldiers, most of whom were African Americans, were considered by some to be the best American unit in Vietnam.

African Americans distinguished themselves in combat. On October 22, 1965, Olive, nicknamed "Preacher" for his habit of quoting from the Bible, covered an enemy grenade with his own body to save four of his comrades. He was killed instantly. "It was the most incredible display of selfless bravery I have ever witnessed," his commanding officer would later say. Milton Olive was

Milton Olive, Jr., with the Medal of Honor awarded posthumously to his son. On either side of President Johnson are two of the four soldiers saved by Olive's heroism.

awarded the Medal of Honor posthumously for his heroism, and the city of Chicago named a park and a junior college after him.

Just two weeks after Olive died, African American Lawrence Joel, also with the Sky Soldiers, earned his own Medal of Honor. Shot twice during a battle that lasted twenty-four hours, Joel refused treatment of his wounds and continued to tend to the fallen comrades around him. Joel's "attention to duty saved a large number of lives," it was later said, "and his unselfish, daring example under most adverse conditions was an inspiration to all."

One night, with only one week left to go of his time in Vietnam, Dwight Johnson's tank platoon commander assigned him to a different tank because another driver was sick. The next day, the tanks were ambushed by enemy soldiers with rockets. Johnson watched in horror as his usual tank was blown up. In a rage, he spent the next half hour singlehandedly repelling the enemy's ambush. Even after he ran out of ammunition, he kept fighting.

Winstel Belton, whose refusal to go to Vietnam with his unit had earned him a court-martial conviction, had convinced his superiors to drop his remaining jail time if he served in Vietnam. One day his unit was ambushed, and the commanding officer's radio was dropped in the confusion.

Belton risked his life to retrieve the radio, earning praise and a recommendation for promotion from the officer.

The demands of combat molded prominent African-American commanders. Charles Rogers, who felt that command of a combat unit was essential to his career, was by now a lieutenant colonel. He commanded an artillery unit situated in the jungle near the Cambodian border. In the early morning hours of November 1, 1968, Rogers led his men in turning back a bloody assault by NVA soldiers, despite being wounded several times. Rogers was awarded the Medal of Honor for his actions, becoming the highest ranking African-American soldier ever to earn the honor.

African-American Brigadier General Frederic E. Davison led the Army's 199th Light Infantry Brigade in combat during 1968 and 1969. Lieutenant Colonel Hurdle Maxwell became the first African American to command a Marine Corps infantry battalion in 1968. Colin Powell, the future general and chairman of the Joint Chiefs of Staff, served two tours with the infantry in Vietnam.

The price for their heavy participation in combat was a high combat casualty rate among African-American soldiers. During one period between 1965 and 1966, one out of every four U.S. soldiers killed in Vietnam was black. Many African

Americans suffered devastating battlefield injuries as well.

Some saw the high casualty rates among African Americans as unfortunate by-products of the progress they had made achieving integration. "I feel good about it," said George Shoffer, an African-American lieutenant colonel in the Army. "Not that I like the bloodshed, but the performance of the Negro in Vietnam tends to offset the fact that the Negro wasn't considered worthy of being a frontline soldier in other wars."

African Americans back in the United States wondered if the integration of the military was an excuse for racist white commanders to use blacks to do most of the fighting. Reporters accompanying combat units had noticed high concentrations of African Americans in the riskiest frontline areas, where they were most likely to engage the enemy. In fact, although African Americans made up only about 12 percent of the national population, it was not uncommon for frontline units to be 30 to 40 percent black, or more.

The percentage of black casualties was reduced by 1967, after the Army and Marine Corps began to assign more African Americans to noncombat duties to ensure fairness. By the end of the war in 1972, the total percentage of black battlefield deaths was 12.1 percent, roughly equal to the

". . . the performance of the Negro in Vietnam tends to offset the fact that the Negro wasn't considered worthy of being a frontline soldier in other wars."

percentage of African Americans in the U.S. population.

In 1965, U.S. aircraft began what was known as Operation Rolling Thunder, in which U.S. aircraft bombed selected targets in North Vietnam in an attempt to halt the flow of communist troops and supplies into South Vietnam. Between 1965 and 1968, approximately 640,000 tons of bombs were dropped on North Vietnam.

As they had in World War II and Korea, African-American pilots performed well in the air war over Vietnam. Lieutenant General Benjamin O. Davis, Jr., one of the original Tuskegee Airmen, commanded the 13th Air Force. The Marines' first African-American pilot, Lieutenant Colonel Frank Peterson, commanded a fighter squadron.

Frank Peterson

Major James T. Boddie, Jr., of Baltimore, Maryland, flew more than 150 missions over North and South Vietnam in his F-4 Phantom jet, earning nine Air Medals. Daniel "Chappie" James, Jr., who would one day become the nation's first African-American four-star general, was second in command of an Air Force fighter wing known as the "Wolfpack." Colonel James flew dozens of missions, including a famous air battle known as Operation Bolo in 1967, in which seven enemy jets were shot down without a single U.S. jet being lost.

During Operation Rolling Thunder, the United States lost 993 aircraft to enemy action. Colonel Fred Cherry, who as a boy in Virginia had dreamed of becoming a pilot, was shot down in his F-105 jet over North Vietnam on October 25, 1965. Of the forty-three Americans who had been captured in the north, Colonel Cherry was the first African American. Cherry was held as a prisoner of war for almost eight years, during which time he was beaten and tortured and spent long periods in solitary confinement. Remarkably, he endured his captivity and refused to allow the enemy to break his will. He was finally released on February 12, 1973.

In Vietnam, African Americans served ably and heroically in a multitude of medical and other support roles crucial to the U.S. war effort. Twenty-year-old Texan Clarence E. Sasser, a medic with the 9th Infantry Division, won the Medal of Honor for saving the lives of injured soldiers despite his own painful injuries.

African-American women such as Juanita C. Forbes of Michigan and Olivia Theriot of Minnesota served as flight nurses in Vietnam. They supervised the evacuation by airplane of injured U.S. soldiers who would receive treatment in hospitals in the United States and Japan. "It isn't easy," Captain Theriot once remarked about the challenge

Clarence E. Sasser

of treating critically injured young men as they left the combat zone behind, "and it takes a while to get used to."

African-American civilians also worked in Vietnam. Often, civilian workers could earn from 25 to 70 percent more at jobs in Vietnam, and many African Americans saw opportunities that weren't available back in the States. Dr. Isaiah A. Jackson, a civilian physician from Richmond, Virginia, treated wounded Vietnamese civilians in a Danang hospital, finding a "sense of fulfillment" in his duties in Vietnam. African-American journalist Wallace Terry covered the war for *Time* magazine from 1967 to 1969. Terry, who accompanied combat units into the thick of battle, later wrote a best-selling book called *Bloods* recounting the experiences of twenty African-American fighting men in Vietnam.

By the end of 1967 there were roughly three hundred thousand African-American men and women in the U.S. armed forces. A large number, almost sixty thousand, were in or near South Vietnam, performing admirably in a wide variety of duties.

From the most decorated hero to the lowliest foot soldier, African Americans were making the most of the opportunity to serve and compete on an equal basis with whites. Like the society they had left behind, however, Vietnam was a place where many African Americans quickly learned that performing one's job well was not always enough to earn the respect of others. The ugly stain of racism had followed African Americans to Southeast Asia.

Chapter 5

No Room for Prejudice

By the end of 1967, the war was going badly for the United States. American combat deaths had increased each year since 1965, and in 1967 almost ten thousand Americans were killed in Vietnam. The Vietcong were waging their deadly guerrilla war in the south. Although the bombing of military targets continued in the north, communist troops and supplies still poured into South Vietnam. Morale was low among U.S. troops, who had expected a quick and decisive victory.

In hearings before Congress in 1966, government officials had been divided over U.S. policy in Vietnam. Despite General Westmoreland's optimistic reports about the progress of the American effort during 1967, it seemed to some that an end to the war was nowhere in sight. Early opponents of U.S. involvement were now joined by an increasingly vocal number of politicians, religious leaders, and members of the media. Students at colleges across America protested the war at rallies and demonstrations.

In January 1968, during the Vietnamese New Year holiday known as Tet, the Vietcong launched a surprise attack on cities and towns throughout South Vietnam, hoping to turn the South Vietnamese against their government. The Tet Offensive, as the attack became known, lasted for several days.

Although the attack ultimately failed, Americans back home were overwhelmed by the graphic scenes of the war they saw each night on the television news. The Vietcong had attacked cities deep within South Vietnam. Clearly they were not an enemy on the verge of defeat, as the U.S. government had assured the American people.

Public opinion about America's involvement in Vietnam grew more negative. The original members of the antiwar movement were now not the only Americans who mistrusted their government's reports on the war. The war effort was proving costly, both in American lives and in money, and yet did not appear to be accomplishing anything. Many Americans felt betrayed, and they spoke out against U.S. participation in the war.

Within the ranks of America's soldiers, another war was brewing, this one between blacks and whites. In the early years of the war, especially among troops involved directly in combat, stories of racial harmony had abounded. Troops in combat depend on one another for their lives. "When you got out in the jungle there was no room for prejudice," recalled Charles Strong.

"The first white friend I had," former Army combat photographer Stephen A. Howard remembered, "I had in Vietnam." African-American Arthur Woodley remembered meeting a white soldier who was a member of the Ku Klux Klan and had never seen a black man before. "He never knew why he hated black people," said Woodley. The two became best friends.

Some black soldiers and white soldiers became friends in Vietnam, despite problems caused by racial prejudice

Friendships forged in the heat of combat could not erase the discrimination and racism that still existed in the military. To many observers, the draft was one example. In 1967, approximately 16 percent of the men drafted were African Americans, despite the fact that blacks made up just over 12 percent of the population. The majority of those drafted ended up in the Army and were sent to Vietnam. "The fighting in Vietnam," stated a government report from 1984, "was thus on the shoulders of a disproportionate number of blacks and other minorities, as well as on the shoulders of [poor] white Americans."

African Americans were also more likely to be subjected to disciplinary action in Vietnam than whites. Indeed, many left the service after Vietnam with "less than honorable" discharges after being punished for misconduct. And they were less likely to be awarded medals in Vietnam than whites. Promotion to higher ranks came slower. In August 1968 there were 1,342 generals and admirals in the U.S. armed forces. Only two, Benjamin O. Davis, Jr., and Frederic E. Davison, were African Americans. Of the more than 400,000 officers in the combined military, only 8,325 were black. This lack of African-American leaders was a sharp contrast to the large number of black soldiers serving at the time.

African Americans were often subjected to racist insults and graffiti. Many found the Confederate flags that were flown in some units offensive because the rebel flag was a symbol of the South that had enslaved black people before the Civil War. In 1967 Clide Brown, a black patrol leader, was featured in a magazine article dealing with race relations in Vietnam. Shortly afterward, a burning cross was placed outside his tent. Although such incidents usually occurred away from the combat zone, their impact was felt throughout the African-American community in Vietnam.

The civil rights movement, which had begun in the 1950s with African Americans protesting Jim Crow laws, had since produced significant legal victories for black people. These included passage of laws against segregation, plus laws guaranteeing the right to vote and to have fair and equal access to housing. In 1964 President Lyndon Johnson, appalled by living conditions among America's poor, had launched his "War on Poverty," which included efforts to provide job training and improved housing for the neediest Americans.

While these efforts improved the lives of some African Americans, they were not enough. African Americans were still subjected to racism and discrimination. For example, when they tried to exercise newly established legal rights in the South, some blacks encountered violence by whites. The overall quality of living conditions, job opportunities, schools, and health care in African-American communities continued to deteriorate.

Many of the black soldiers who fought in the early years of the war were career men like Ed Huff or Ollie Henderson, Sr., who in 1966 had already been in the Army for twenty-two years. Such career soldiers had little involvement with the civil rights movement back home, and they often treated racism as if it did not exist. "The main thing to do is to do our job and get out of this damned country," said Joseph Conner, an African-American sergeant in the Army. "Civil rights can wait, as far as soldiers are concerned."

Others considered their success in the military itself to be part of the battle for justice and equality. "If you're at the top," Daniel "Chappie" James, Jr., liked to say, "you don't have to plead the way you do if you're at the bottom." Sometimes criticized by African Americans back home for selling out to the white man, leaders like James saw themselves as pioneers, opening doors to new opportunities for African Americans.

As the war dragged on, however, many of the African-American career soldiers came home, to be replaced by younger troops. These new soldiers were far more likely to be draftees, straight from the cities and towns of a changing America. Their attitudes toward racism, and the war itself, had been shaped by dramatic events both in Vietnam and at home.

In the mid-sixties, after hundreds of years of oppression at the hands of white America, black frustration and rage boiled over. Between 1965 and 1967 racially motivated riots wreaked havoc in America's cities. African Americans in Vietnam were distressed by news that their cities were burning. Many condemned the violence as the work of hoodlums. Some feared that after leaving Vietnam they would be used as riot control troops against their own people.

President Johnson, whose plan for improving the quality of American life was called "The Great Society," appointed a special commission to study the problem of racial violence in America. The commission considered such things as housing, education, job opportunity, medical care, crime rates, and other areas, and it found a "clear pattern of severe disadvantage for Negroes."

Faced with the failure of America's elected leaders to bring social justice to their people, many black leaders called for independent action among African Americans to improve their quality of life. Emphasizing pride in African-American culture, the "Black Power" movement urged African

Americans to stop waiting for whites to change and to take their welfare into their own hands.

To some, the desperate situation of black America called for immediate—and violent, if necessary—resistance to white oppression. For militant groups like the Black Panther Party in California and leaders such as Stokely Carmichael, violence was a means of "liberation" from oppression. Carmichael advocated "guerrilla warfare" in the nation's ghettoes.

Sending so many African Americans to fight in far-off Vietnam amid such racial tension and anger at home fueled more protest. A national opinion poll had shown that 35 percent of African Americans in the United States opposed the war in 1966. By 1969, the number opposing the war had reached almost 70 percent. Many African Americans feared that the progress of the civil rights movement and the social programs of the Great Society would be overlooked—and not adequately funded—as a result of the expensive U.S. commitment in Vietnam.

Black Muslim leader Malcolm X had begun speaking out against the war in 1964. He criticized the U.S. government for sending black soldiers to Vietnam to fight for democracy when African Americans in the American South were victimized by violence simply trying to register to vote. "If it is wrong to be violent defending Black women and Black children," he argued, " . . . then it is wrong for America to draft us and make us violent in defense of her."

In 1966, national civil rights groups began to protest against the war. Nobel Peace Prize winner Dr. Martin Luther King, Jr., a central figure in the civil rights movement, became a vocal critic of American policy in Vietnam. "We are taking young black men who have been crippled by our society," he said, "and sending them 8,000 miles away to guarantee liberties in Southeast Asia which they have not found in Southwest Georgia or in East Harlem."

Dr. King was criticized by some civil rights leaders who believed that the issues of civil rights and the war in Vietnam should be dealt with separately. Even so, he continued to speak out against the war. King justified his antiwar activities by pointing out that the enormous cost of the war drained money away from the national government that should be spent assisting poor African Americans at home.

Other voices of protest were more forceful. "We want all black men to be exempt from military service," declared the Black Panthers, who considered the Vietnamese victims of "the white racist government of America." Eldridge Cleaver, noting

Eldridge Cleaver

the high number of black casualties in Vietnam, charged that "the United States government is sending all those black troops to Vietnam . . . to kill off the cream of black youth."

Many African-American soldiers entering the military for the first time in 1968 had strong opinions about such things as the unfairness of the draft, the high numbers of blacks killed in combat, and racial incidents in Vietnam. Having witnessed hard-fought civil rights battles back in the United States, they were unwilling to put up with racism and discrimination as they fought a foreign war for America. This new breed of African-American soldier "called for unity among black brothers on the battlefield," according to journalist Wallace Terry, "to protest these indignities and provide mutual support. And they called themselves 'Bloods.'"

"Bloods," short for "blood brothers," banded together to protect one another from racism. "A lot of times all we had was each other," remembered Reginald Edwards. "It was like everybody was against us." Bloods supported each other by studying black history and culture together. "Brothers really, really stuck together," Edwards continued. "I've never seen them stick together like that again. 'Brother' really meant something."

Many African Americans in Vietnam had a

special way of greeting one another known as the "dap." The dap was a series of handshakes and grips that signified togetherness and brotherhood. "The dap," Edwards fondly recalled, " . . . was so together. We had to have our own handshake. It was so special." The Army did its best to prohibit African American soldiers from using the dap.

On April 4, 1968, Dr. King was assassinated by a white man in Memphis, Tennessee. Racial tension between blacks and whites exploded as never before in American history. Riots in 169 U.S. cities caused over $130 million in property damage and claimed forty-three lives. In Chicago, entire city blocks were burned down. When National Guard troops were ordered into Washington, D.C., to restore calm, militant black leaders urged African Americans to arm themselves. "When the white man comes," said Stokely Carmichael, "he is going to kill you."

African Americans in Vietnam were stunned by the news of King's death. "When I heard that Martin Luther King was assassinated," said Don F. Browne, who served as a military policeman with the Air Force in Saigon, "my first inclination was to run out and punch the first white guy I saw. I was very hurt. All I wanted to do was to go home."

"I happened to live in an all black hut,"

remembered Randolph Doby. "It was the first all black hut in Vietnam. And there were eight of us in that hut. And it was interesting that even before we knew that he had been killed, all of a sudden all these Confederate flags started flying over a lot of quonset huts, and some of the major facilities."

The Vietcong attempted to exploit the anger and frustration of African-Americans. "To play on the sympathy of the black soldier," stated Browne, "the Viet Cong would shoot at a white guy, then let the black guy behind him go through, then shoot at the next white guy."

Communist propaganda tried to turn black soldiers against their white comrades. The sign reads: "U.S. Negr (sic) Armymen! You are committing the same ignominious crimes in South Vietnam (blank) that the KKK clique is perpetrating against your family at home."

African-American aviator Norman Alexander McDaniel's jet had been shot down in 1966. He was being held as a prisoner of war (POW) in North Vietnam at the time that Martin Luther King was killed. He had grown up in segregated Fayetteville, North Carolina. As a youngster Mc-Daniel had lived under Jim Crow, riding in the back of the bus and attending inferior, segregated schools.

"When Dr. King was assassinated," he remembered, "they called me in for interrogation to see if I would make a statement critical of the United States . . . . they wanted me to tell black soldiers not to fight because the United States is waging a war of genocide, using dark-skinned people against dark-skinned people. I would tell them no."

King's death caused many African-American soldiers to lose faith that the military, or America, would try to change. Some became increasingly militant in their attitudes toward whites and the war, separating themselves from whites and showing disdain for authority. They raised clenched fists as a salute to black power and flew flags of red, black, and green as a symbol of liberation.

Between 1968 and 1972, there were hundreds of racial incidents within the U.S. military. Some were organized protests such as rallies and mass demonstrations. Some involved soldiers refusing to follow orders or staging "sit-ins." Not limited strictly to Vietnam, many of these incidents took place at military bases in the United States, Germany, and wherever American soldiers were stationed.

Sometimes racial incidents led to violence. Race riots, such as the one at the Army jail at Long Binh in August 1968, left black and white soldiers dead or injured. Racial assaults were reported at military bases throughout the United States. The Navy, which had the smallest percentage of African Americans, had incidents on some of its ships, including a fifteen-hour fight between blacks and whites on the USS *Kittyhawk*.

Military leaders sent a committee to Vietnam in 1969 to investigate racial problems. The group reported a "dangerous situation" needing immediate attention. The Defense Department issued orders aimed at eliminating unequal treatment of African Americans, in an attempt to improve relations between the races in the military.

The Army eased its restrictions on Afro-style haircuts. The dap was no longer prohibited. Integrated commissions were set up to deal with racial complaints, and African-American history and culture courses were offered to interested soldiers. Beginning in 1971, with America's war in Vietnam winding down, every single member of the armed forces was required to attend classes in race relations. The program was, in the words of African-American Pentagon official L. Howard Bennett, "one of the most significant things the Defense Department has ever done" with regard to race relations.

The most dramatic changes came in the Navy. "In less than three years," recalled African-American William S. Norman, who reported on race problems to the Navy's senior admiral, "we instituted some 200 new programs. We had a new Navy. The first ships were named after black heroes. The first black was promoted to admiral. Ten percent of our NROTC [officer training] units were set aside for predominantly black colleges. We guaranteed that blacks would be on promotion boards, assignment boards, and would make their way to the command colleges."

For many of the African Americans who served in Vietnam, however, such changes were coming far too late. Whether they believed in America's cause there or simply fought because they had no choice, most black fighting men had seen racism firsthand in Vietnam even as they risked their lives for their country. Of those who managed to come home alive, some faced greater struggles and injustices ahead.

Chapter 6

A Special Price

By the end of 1968, many Americans no longer cared whether the communists controlled all of Vietnam. Thirty thousand Americans had died there. Billions of dollars had already been spent waging the war. That year, Richard M. Nixon had been elected president after promising the American people he had a secret way to end the conflict.

In Vietnam, the antiwar movement and racial strife back home were having a negative impact on the morale of American troops. Reacting to the frustration of the war and the turnabout in American public opinion after the Tet Offensive, U.S. soldiers now began to see the war as a no-win situation. None wanted to die in a lost cause. In some units, search-and-destroy became "search-and-avoid." Some soldiers refused to obey orders to continue fighting. Officers grew wary of their troops as stories of "fraggings" became more common. A fragging was the killing of an officer by his own soldiers, either because they felt the officer jeopardized their safety through incompetence or because they felt he was untrustworthy.

Despite his pledge to end America's involvement in Vietnam, President Nixon still attempted to force the communists to give up their cause. In 1968 and again in 1969, the Air Force conducted more heavy bombing missions over Vietnam than in all of the previous years of the war combined. Almost ten thousand Americans died in Vietnam in 1969. Despite this, there was no doubt that the United States was disengaging itself from Vietnam. One way or another, America was getting out.

A former POW is welcomed home by his wife

Most U.S. soldiers spent one year in Vietnam. As a result, throughout the duration of the war, tens of thousands of U.S. servicemen and women had already left Vietnam, coming home one at a time. Many African Americans chose to continue their military careers, even opting for additional tours in Vietnam. For career men like Ed Huff and Medal of Honor winner Charles Rogers, the choice was easy. They were "lifers," and retirement was the only way they would leave the armed forces.

Huff, the first African-American sergeant major in the Marine Corps, retired in 1972 as the senior enlisted man in the entire armed forces. "That's a long way to come," he said, "for a boy who came into the Marines so poor he had just a quarter in his pocket." Returning from Vietnam in 1969, Charles Rogers continued to advance in the Army, eventually becoming a two-star general. He retired in 1985 and became a minister.

Between 1966 and 1967, almost half the African Americans eligible for discharge elected to stay in the armed forces. At one point during the war, African Americans in the Navy, Air Force, and Marines reenlisted at twice the rate of white soldiers; three times as many reenlisted in the Army. Many believed in America's cause in Vietnam and wanted to see the job they had begun through to the end. Others were tempted by the promise of a hefty reenlistment bonus.

Other African Americans stayed in the service because of the opportunities for success it offered compared to what was available back home. David Tuck, the radio operator from Cleveland, said, "Some black soldiers I know are reenlisting, but that shows how bad the society is for black people—that they should have to stay in the Army to find a decent life."

When the first big troop withdrawals began in 1969, there were already over one hundred twenty thousand African-American Vietnam veterans. Government reports from 1968 portrayed the typical African-American veteran as being about twenty-two years old, a high school graduate, and more interested in continuing his education after the war than most white veterans. In fact, over one half of all African-American veterans were reported to be taking advantage of government programs such as the "GI Bill," a law that provides benefits to veterans who want to continue their schooling.

The vast majority of African American soldiers were able to successfully make the transition to civilian life. As a group, they tended to be better educated than blacks who had not served in the military. They also tended to earn more in civilian jobs once they came home, despite the fact that most had very little job experience before shipping out to Vietnam. Many took advantage of a government program called "Project Transition," which provided counseling, job training, and job placement for interested veterans.

By 1992, African-American veterans Charles Strong and Robert Holcomb both owned businesses in Florida. Reginald Edwards, who had joined the Black Panthers after coming home from Vietnam, worked as the art director for the United Black Fund. "I miss the comradery of the brothers," he said of Vietnam, " . . . the way we stuck together in 'Nam was like the most beautiful thing I ever experienced."

Robert Mountain, whose foot was amputated after an incoming mortar shell ripped into him one night in Vietnam, was fitted with an artificial limb. He earned his college degree and began counseling other amputees in veterans' hospitals. He also began running, competing in track events for amputees, and before retiring from competition in 1985 had set world records for speed. Asked if he would fight for America again, Mountain replied that he would. "I can't enjoy all of the liberties that we have rights to in America," he said, "and call myself a black American and say this is my land and not be willing to support her in war or time of need."

Many African-American veterans ended up working with other veterans. Harold Bryant was the membership director for the National Association of Black Veterans. He spent the first year and a half home from Vietnam on unemployment, then decided to go back to school. Noticing the large number of unemployed African-American veterans around him, he began a veterans' assistance project at his university and has been involved in veterans' affairs ever since.

"I just want to be remembered as a man who went and did what he had to do to come back home to his family," Bryant said. "Didn't declare against the war. Didn't run off. Looked upon it as what it was—stop communism from spreading, and doing what was asked of him as an American."

In 1993, African-American Marine veteran Jesse Brown was chosen by President Bill Clinton to serve as secretary of veterans' affairs. Brown was wounded while on patrol in Vietnam in 1965.

The war had cost the United States over $150 billion, hurting the U.S. economy and making jobs for returning veterans scarce. Despite programs like the GI Bill and Project Transition, many African-American veterans encountered tough economic times upon their return. In many black communities the unemployment rate was three times the national average. For African Americans between the ages of twenty and twenty-five, the unemployment rate sometimes went as high as eight or nine times the national average.

Charles Cato came home to find that his old job as a jeweler's apprentice was no longer available. "Things are slow now," he was told by his former boss. Despite his willingness to work, Cato was forced to collect unemployment insurance from the government.

"Race is still the major factor when you look for a job," said Arthur Caree, an African American who served as a radar specialist on a Navy aircraft carrier. "I went to several electronics plants back home," he said, "and they tried to stick a broom in my hand."

The employment problem was compounded by the fact that although 97 percent of all soldiers who served in Vietnam received honorable discharges, of the 3 percent that didn't, a large number were African-Americans. "Bad paper," as less-than-honorable discharges were known, made it even harder for black veterans to find jobs.

While they prepared to come home, many African-American soldiers had voiced concerns about their status once back in America. After combat, few were prepared to tolerate second-class status as civilians. "I don't think I'm going to have as much patience as I had before when I go home," said the Navy's Joe Jones. "Why should I? There are some things due me and I want them." Ollie Henderson voiced similar feelings. "I feel right now I've qualified myself for anything anybody else has," he said. "I've exposed myself to the same dangers."

Some returning black veterans could not help feeling bitter about the racism that persisted in America. During the late 1960s the civil rights movement and the Great Society had been pushed aside by the war. Legal victories over segregation and discrimination often seemed hollow amid the decreasing quality of life in America's urban ghettos.

"The brother in Vietnam closed his eyes to the prejudice he knew existed and hoped against hope that America would change, would change because he fought for her," said Ahmed Lorenc, an African-American marine. "But it didn't make a bit of difference, not a bit."

Militant black groups appealed to the anger of some African-American veterans. David Tuck became an activist in the Black Anti-Draft Union in Cleveland, Ohio, where he attempted to persuade African Americans to resist the draft in any way they could. "I would never fight on a foreign shore for America again," he said. "The only place

I would fight is right here. Black people should not be called upon to assume the duties of citizenship when they don't enjoy the rights and privileges."

In the past, American veterans returning from war have been honored as heroes and patriots. For Vietnam veterans, however, particularly those who came home after 1968, it was different. America had lost her first war. The war had been unpopular and had bitterly divided people. Politicians and military leaders had lost the confidence of the people. And most importantly, tens of thousands of Americans had lost their lives in a futile cause. For many returning veterans, it was as if they were to blame.

"I didn't come home to no band playing," recalled Arthur Woodley. In fact, many Americans ignored the returning soldiers. "When I got back to the real world," said Robert Mountain, "it seemed nobody cared that you'd been to Vietnam." The lack of recognition for their sacrifice confused and angered many veterans. "A lot of Vietnam veterans that I know are still disappointed with our nation," said Mountain years later. "I see a lot of brothers who are still largely, largely disappointed."

Veterans who weren't ignored were sometimes treated as if there was something wrong with them.

"For the most part," said Dwight Edwards, an African-American former Army paratrooper, "we were looked upon as baby killers, drug addicts, malcontents, and any other kind of negative concept that you had." Indeed, in the years since the war, images of crazed, gun-wielding Vietnam veterans going berserk in civilian society have been a common theme in books, television shows, and movies about the war.

Many veterans did suffer from a variety of problems related to the war. As many as a half million may have been exposed to Agent Orange, a chemical sprayed from airplanes to kill foliage, resulting in cancer and birth defects in their children. Over

American planes sprayed chemicals to kill foliage which hid the Vietcong from sight

three hundred thousand American men and women were injured in Vietnam—nearly a third of these were left with severe disabilities. Sergeant Robert Daniels, an African-American artillery gunner from Chicago, suffered severe burns and lost his hand when a mine exploded beneath a vehicle he was in. After months in the hospital he came home and spent two years looking for a job. "I got discouraged," he said later. "I guess I just gave up, because I kept getting turned down."

Drug and alcohol abuse in Vietnam left scars on many veterans as well. The Defense Department estimated that between 1968 and 1972 approximately 60 percent of U.S. soldiers used marijuana, while 30 percent used narcotics such as heroin. As many as 20 percent of all enlisted men in Vietnam were addicted to narcotics in 1970. A 1981 government report found that among combat soldiers there was also a high rate of alcoholism, even for many who had never used alcohol heavily before the war. Many brought these problems home with them.

Such addictions made the transition to civilian life all the more difficult. In 1990, a government study revealed that African-American veterans aged twenty and older had an unemployment rate that was double the national average. Many of these are veterans of Vietnam. Without jobs these veterans are unable to enjoy the things most Americans take for granted. For example, half of the nation's homeless veterans are African Americans.

Many who served in Vietnam suffer even today from psychological problems related to stress, depression, and severe anger. Some saw or did things in Vietnam that made coming home and living a normal life very difficult. One of the most tragic stories is that of tank driver Dwight Johnson. Home from Vietnam in July 1968, Johnson looked for but could not find a job. Then, in November, he was awarded the Medal of Honor for his gallantry the year before, when his tank platoon had been ambushed. Once he received the medal, Johnson became quite popular. Several job offers came his way. He eventually returned to the Army as a recruiter. But Johnson was plagued by personal problems, including difficulty dealing with the attention the Medal of Honor brought and guilt over his experience in Vietnam. His life slowly went out of control. On April 30, 1971, he was shot and killed by a clerk as he tried to rob a liquor store.

In February 1973, a peace agreement was signed ending America's involvement in the Vietnam War. Within a month, the last U.S. combat troops had departed the country. A mere two years later, in the spring of 1975, the communists swept through South Vietnam to locations just outside Saigon, the capital city. South Vietnam's appeals to the United States for military assistance had gone unanswered. Congress was unwilling to become involved in Vietnam again. On April 30, 1975, as thousands of panicked South Vietnamese tried to get out of the city, a U.S. helicopter rescued the last remaining American employees of the American embassy in Saigon. The North Vietnamese entered and captured the city, raising their flag over the embassy where the U.S. flag had flown. The war was over.

Despite the problems experienced by many, most African Americans who served in Vietnam were able to resume their lives after the war with little or no difficulty. These veterans had served their country well, even while fighting for a losing cause. On top of all the hardship and turmoil of Vietnam, however, having to deal with racism both during and after the war was a cruel blow. "Vietnam left a scar on them that won't go away," said William Norman of his fellow African-American fighting men and women. "The black soldier paid a special price."

Chapter 7

This Is My Country

On November 8, 1992, in preparation for Veterans Day, a crowd of people gathered by the Vietnam Veterans Memorial in Washington, D.C. "The Wall," as it has become known, was ten years old. Since 1982 over thirty million people had visited the five-hundred-foot black *V* with the names of all 58,183 Americans killed or missing in Vietnam inscribed upon it. Many had left mementos in honor of friends or family members whose names are carved into the polished granite. Others simply touched the names, or traced them onto paper as their own memento. Now, almost twenty years after the end of America's longest war, volunteers began to read the names aloud, one by one.

The memorial at the Wall symbolized long-overdue recognition of the sacrifices Americans made in Vietnam. After years of denial, resentment, and anger over what happened there, many of the

CHARLES J MURPHY Jr · BURTON K McCORD · D
LE[...]S M THOMAS · ROBERT L VADEN · CHARLES
RA[...]H H LIVESAY · JOHN A McCURDY · ROBERT
V[...]TER H ANDERSON · ANTHONY J BATTISTA · [...]
[...]EN D GRETHEN · TONY H HUGHES · JAMES H
[...]HAEL J McGOLDRICK · JOHN PARNELLA · JAM[...]
[...]RENCE A TEAS · TOMMIE MAX CRIPE · THOM[...]
[...]YNE H ROWLAND · GEORGE E RUTLEDGE · LY[...]
[...]NNY A BOLIN · THOMAS H CARUTHERS · GERA[...]
[...]ILLIAM T MAIN · LEE A ADAMS · JOSEPH O BRO[...]
[...]ARRELL Z MAGRUDER · A D MOSLEY · BENNETT[...]
[...]N ABBOTT · FAMOUS L LANE · LAWRENCE V P[...]
[...]GE J SKAPINSKY · GROVER R TAYLOR · ROY D[...]
[...]LES R GURTLER · MICHAEL W HEUER · JACK [...]
[...]NORRIS · DANIEL L P SAUVE · WILLIAM[...]
[...]MON · MIGUEL GARCIA Jr · CLYDE HA[...]
[...]BOTT · JAMES E COOK · FRANCISCO C[...]
[...]SAACS · GERALD B KASPRZYK · LARRY F W[...]
[...]TERWILLIGER · WILLIAM E COOPER · DO[...]
[...]HALL · HENRY PANGELINAN PEREDA · R[...]
[...]N · KENNETH E TURNER · DAVID[...]
[...]ARL STANLEY · RICHARD M LIN[...]
[...]WILLIAM L WALTON · GEOR[...]

"At our very best,
Americans move past
division and heal."

wounds the war opened have begun to heal. The bitter divisions caused by America's failed policy in Vietnam have given way, however slowly, to a quiet acceptance of the fact that most Americans, whether politicians, generals, protesters, or foot soldiers, tried to do right thing in Vietnam. "At our very best," said African-American leader Jesse Jackson in a speech before the Wall, "Americans move past division and heal."

For African Americans, the war has left a complicated, bittersweet legacy. Forever erased on the battlefields of Vietnam was the notion that African Americans cannot fight, lead, or work together as well as whites. Whatever the merits of the struggle they engaged in, the leadership, ability, bravery, and patriotism of the black fighting men and women of Vietnam will echo through American history as the proud triumph of a people finally allowed to participate as equals.

African-American heroes and role models emerged from the war, demonstrating how to overcome adversity and injustice in one's life as Edgar Huff did. Most simply came home and resumed their places as citizens, family members, and contributors to the rich fabric of American society. Perhaps the best known, General Colin Powell, became the senior military leader in the United States and led the country through the war in the

Persian Gulf. "Whenever I see that brother, I want to stand up at attention," said Harold Bryant, "'cause I know what he had to put up with to get where he is."

For many African-American veterans, however, the legacy of Vietnam is altogether negative. Lingering physical problems, drug and alcohol addiction, unemployment, homelessness, and hopelessness have taken their toll on far too many of the survivors. These veterans are in dire need of healing.

Even as it struggled in Vietnam, America struggled toward a new understanding of racial equality. For the African-American fighting man, this struggle often became a war within a war. As he made the most of opportunities in Vietnam—to serve, to fight, to lead—the African-American soldier also felt the sting of discrimination and racism. Some grew demoralized and bitter. Others demanded that their equality be acknowledged, changing forever the status of African Americans in the military.

In the years since Vietnam, however, American society has sometimes seemed to go backward in racial matters. Legal rights have not been a guarantee against subtle forms of racism in virtually all aspects of society, including the armed forces. "It's invisible," said one African-American soldier, "but you feel the racism of a lot of the white guys. The whites are still top dog and the brothers know it."

Some African Americans have shunned the American dream that seems not to include them. Arthur Woodley spoke for many when he said, "Vietnam is not over for me yet. I'm just a lost warrior. I just don't have the weapons to fight back with. The enemy is the same system I fought for."

Many black veterans feel that their achievements have yet to be recognized and celebrated. "We're still invisible men," said Harold Bryant. "I want us to be remembered in books," he continued. "Films. Television shows. To educate the masses as to what our contributions have been."

Knowing that America is far from perfect, countless African-American Vietnam veterans still take great pride in America and their contributions to her during the war. Like Daniel "Chappie" James, Jr., before his death in 1978, they remain hopeful that America will change. "This is my country and I believe in her," he wrote while still in Vietnam. "If she has any ills, I'll stand by her and hold her hand until in God's given time— through her wisdom and her consideration for the welfare of the entire nation—things are made right again."

A statue near "The Wall" honors America's Vietnam War veterans

Chronology:

African Americans in the U.S. Armed Forces

1770	On March 5, Crispus Attucks, a former slave, is among the first to die in the "Boston Massacre."
1776-1781	7,000 African-American soldiers and sailors take part in the Revolutionary War.
1776	On January 16, the Continental Congress agrees to enlist free blacks.
1812-1815	Black soldiers and sailors fight against the British troops at such critical battles as Lake Erie and New Orleans.
1862-1865	186,000 African-American soldiers serve in black regiments during the Civil War; 38,000 black soldiers lose their lives in more than 400 battles.
1862	On July 17, the U.S. Congress approves the enlistment of black soldiers.
1865	On March 13, the Confederate States of America begins to accept black recruits.
1866-1890	Units of black soldiers, referred to as Buffalo Soldiers, are formed as part of the U.S. Army.
1872	On September 21, John H. Conyers becomes the first African American admitted to the U.S. Naval Academy.
1877	On June 15, Henry O. Flipper becomes the first African American to graduate from West Point.
1914-1918	More than 400,000 African Americans serve in the U.S. armed forces during the First World War.

On May 15, two black soldiers, Henry Johnson and Needham Roberts become the first Americans to receive the French Medal of Honor (*croix de guerre*).	**1918**
In June, Benjamin O. Davis, Jr., graduates from West Point, the first black American to do so in the twentieth century.	**1936**
Benjamin O. Davis, Sr., becomes the first African-American general in the active Regular Army.	**1940**
American forces in World War II include more than a million African-American men and women.	**1941-1945**
On March 25, the Army Air Corps forms its first black unit, the 99th Pursuit Squadron.	**1941**
On August 24, Colonel Benjamin O. Davis, Jr., is made commander of the 99th Pursuit Squadron.	**1942**
On January 27 and 28, the airmen of the 99th Pursuit Squadron score a major victory against enemy fighters at the Italian seaside town of Anzio.	**1944**
On February 2, President Harry S Truman signs Executive Order 9981, ordering an end to segregation in the U.S. armed forces.	**1948**
Black and white forces fight side by side in Korea as separate black fighting units are disbanded.	**1950-1953**
Twenty African-American soldiers are awarded the Congressional Medal of Honor during the Vietnam War.	**1965-1973**
On April 28, Samuel L. Gravely becomes the first black admiral in the history of the U.S. Navy.	**1971**
In August, Daniel "Chapppie" James becomes the first African American to achieve the rank of four-star general.	**1975**
On October 3, Colin Powell becomes the first African-American chairman of the Joint Chiefs of Staff.	**1989**
100,000 African-American men and women are sent to the Middle East during the Persian Gulf conflict.	**1990-1991**
On July 25, the Buffalo Soldier Monument is dedicated at Fort Leavenworth, Kansas.	**1992**

Index

Bibliography

Crane, Elaine, and David, Fay. *The Black Soldier: From the American Revolution to Vietnam.* New York: William Morrow and Company, Inc., 1971.

Doyle, Edward, and Lipsman, Samuel, et al. *The Vietnam Experience* (series). Boston: Boston Publishing Company, 1982.

"The Great Society—In Uniform." *Newsweek*, August 22, 1966.

Johnson, Thomas A. "Negroes in 'The Nam.'" *Ebony*, August, 1968.

Johnson, Thomas A. "Negro Veteran is Confused and Bitter." *New York Times*, July 29, 1968.

Mullen, Robert W. *Blacks in America's Wars: The Shift in Attitudes from the Revolutionary War to Vietnam.* New York: Anchor Found, 1974.

Murphy, Edward F. *Vietnam Medal of Honor Heroes.* New York: Ballantine Books, 1987.

Office of the Deputy Assistant Secretary of Defense for Civilian Personnel Policy/Equal Opportunity. *Black Americans in Defense of Our Nation.* Washington, D.C.: U.S. Government Printing Office, 1991.

"Samaritans on Wings." *Ebony*, May, 1970.

Terry, Wallace. *Bloods: An Oral History of the Vietnam War by Black Veterans.* New York: Ballantine Books, 1992.

"The Bloods of 'Nam." Episode of the WGBH Educational Foundation series "Frontline."